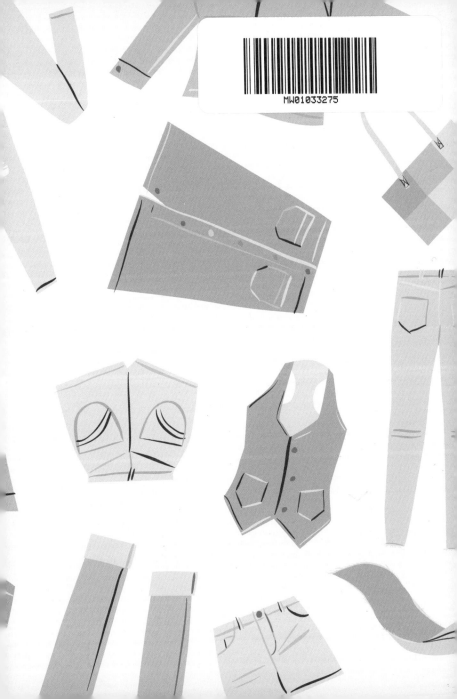

MW01033275

THE ART

of

DENIM

Hardie Grant

BOOKS

CONTENTS

Step in and slide up: *The Art of Denim* unbuttons the story of the world's most iconic fabric from its American frontier to modern times, revealing the most flattering fits and styles, plus the world's very best denim brands from indie jeans-makers to the most exciting vintage labels to look out for in thrift stores and flea markets.

Discover more than 30 ways to wear your true blues, and why women like Cindy Crawford, Drew Barrymore and Missy Elliott are inspirational denim icons.

THIS IS THE ART OF DENIM, ALL ZIPPED UP.

BLUE JEANS UNZIPPED

How denim became our most beloved fabric

Blue jeans are as American as Easy Cheese. First worn by cowboys and rodeo stars, gold miners and railroad workers, jeans became the go-to uniform for civil rights fighters, greasers, beatniks and punks. Today, they're the ultimate casualwear staple that almost everyone has in their wardrobe.

Jeans have earned themselves a permanent place in contemporary global style – and they make your butt look uh-mazing.

They've graced the plump cheeks of Bruce Springsteen on his *Born in the USA* cover, they've been encrusted with rhinestones for Dolly Parton, and they super-powered Britney and Justin's red carpet look in 2001 (when the world was a simpler place). Behind it all is denim, the hardwearing cotton fabric found in almost every wardrobe in the world.

The true origins of denim are hazy at best – and it's not quite as all-American as you think. Not many can agree on the fabric's true origin: was it a pre-17th century wool or silk fabric known as serge de Nimes from Nimes, France? Or an English twill fabric know as Nim? And what about the origin of the word 'jean' that many believe refers to a fabric from Genoa, Italy, a century before? Both were strong and durable, and – as these fabrics and names evolved – by the 1700s, denim stood out. A pure cotton fabric, stronger than jean, denim was made from one coloured thread and one white – and little has changed. Fabric mills in the US started to make denim in the late 1700s, outfitting the pioneers who chased the American Dream, and brands like Levi's® and Lee® were among the first to fashion the workwear fabric into jeans, jackets, and overalls – and the rest is history.

In many ways, denim is just as it always was: coloured and white cotton threads are woven two (or more) over one creating a tough diagonal ribbed structure with coloured thread on top and white on the reverse. Traditionally, the coloured threads are dyed using indigo, a plant-based dye that gives a rich, dark, deep blue hue and, as the fabric wears down, the pale white insides start to show. Pure cotton selvage denim – where an edge to stop unravelling is incorporated into the fabric – is thought to be the gold standard.

Over the years, new ways to make (and wear) denim have kept the fabric fresh and relevant. From the sun-faded denim of the 70s with its bellbottoms and patches, to the wonderfully nasty stonewashes of the 80s, and the bootcut styles of the 90s and 00s. In modern times, almost anything goes, only wearers are increasingly interested in even more flattering fits, clever optical washes to add the illusion of shape, rare Japanese denim created on vintage looms, and clever organic processes that use little water.

The best thing about denim? It becomes part of you. Start with something simple, refined and pared-down and watch how transforms with the little creases and cuts, scrapes and subtle abrasions of the everyday. Your jeans become a map of your life, where you've been and what you've done: a wearable history.

Denim, Unzipped

The magical cotton fabric, made with indigo-dyed and natural coloured yarns, comes in many, many flavours. Here's a few to unbutton at your leisure:

DRY DENIM

Unwashed, unadulterated, dry-feel denim without going through the laundry process – not even a quick rinse. A denim geek favourite, many hold off that first wash as long as possible – months, even years – so that some of the indigo washes away leaving a unique pair of jeans with scuffs and wear-marks.

RIGID DENIM

Denim made of 100 per cent cotton, without any stretch, giving it an authentic, vintage look. Best for wide leg, loose and boyfriend styles.

STRETCH DENIM

A tiny bit of stretch, just two per cent, can make a pair of jeans infinitely more comfortable. Usually, just the weft (the inside yarn) is a blend with stretch capabilities, leaving the warp (the blue outside yarn) looking authentic. Watch out for brands that have great recovery – no one wants to end up with baggy knees.

SELVAGE DENIM

Selvage is a denim fabric (usually) woven on antique shuttle looms with a coloured yarn at the edge to prevent unravelling. The original denim brands like Lee® and Levis® would have a branded colour – Lee® had a green or yellow selvage line, for example.

THE LAUNDRIES

Denim laundries tweak and tune-up raw, dry denim on an industrial scale meaning your jeans may have already been through the works. Pumice stone washes, resin coatings, laser distressing, or bashed into softness with rubber balls: the possibilities are endless. In the end, the best washes are the ones artfully done.

selvage denim

Key Styles

SKINNY

The leg lengthening, curve-accentuating classic stretch denim jeans with snap-back recovery and a jaw-to-floor rear view. Skinny from hip to hem, often slightly cropped or slightly long for a little scrunching around the ankle.

SUPER SKINNY

Ultra-skinny jeans – usually made with a high-stretch fabric – and a regular waist for comfort. Slick super skinny fit, often with a slightly shorter leg for ankle-flashing.

SLIM

Slim and flattering with a subtly higher waist. The most versatile, wear-with-anything fit. Stretch or rigid denim.

STRAIGHT

Simple, straight leg fit with long rise, straight leg, and comfort-shaped waist. Stretch or rigid denim.

BOYFRIEND

A feminine version of the classic men's slim, relaxed fit; stolen from your boyfriend's bedroom floor – and sold on eBay.

BOOTCUT

Usually a regular top half, a skinny fit (so your butt looks great), and cute boot cut – a mini-flare at the bottom. Because, why not?

RELAXED

A slimmed down version of the baggy, high rise jean worn by every suburban mum in the 90s – with a super-flattering straight leg. Slim, not skinny, with a little room up top.

Reclaimed, Reconstructed Denim

THEN ADD:

typographic necklace

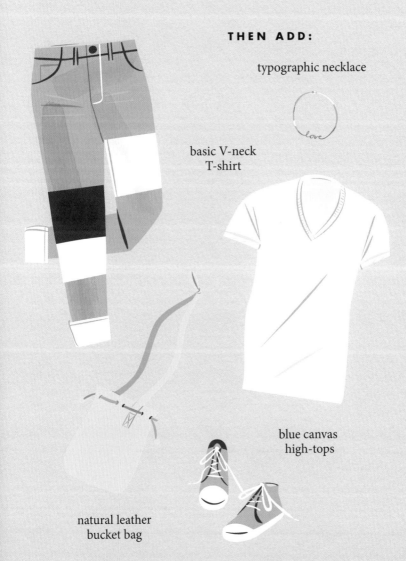

basic V-neck
T-shirt

blue canvas
high-tops

natural leather
bucket bag

Pocketed Denim Jumpsuit

colourfully striped
camisole

woven seagrass
shoulder bag

canvas boat shoes

Distressed Denim Workshirt

THEN ADD:

fisherman's cap

boxy, black leather
handbag

light-wash
vintage
buttonfly
jeans

black leather ankle booties

Style Icon

CINDY CRAWFORD

The most super of supermodels, Cindy Crawford (b. 1966) is the honey-haired, beauty-spotted cover star with a PhD in off-duty glamour and legs for days. In the mid-80s, the onetime chemical engineering student discovered modelling, moved to NYC, and fast-tracked her way to supermodel status throughout the late 80s and 90s with countless runway appearances and mag covers including *Vogue*, *W*, *Harper's Bazaar* and *Allure*.

Crawford's fashion moments include her nude Herb Ritts *Playboy* shoots in 88 and 98; *Freedom 90*, the legendary George Michael music video; her iconic red Versace dress (worn to the Academy Awards in 1991), a white tank and denim shorts for a Pepsi commercial, and her eye-popping leotard looks from her fitness videos.

In the 90s, Crawford wore long rise, stonewash Levi's® and cute cut-offs with white shirts and vest tops in a hot take on the all-American girl. Today her souped-up, sexy take on the classic preppy look is still underpinned by denim. In fact, in 2017 she collaborated with US brand Re/Done on her own range of jeans. With denim part of her fashion history, Crawford now makes simple wide leg jeans worn with vest tops, sandals and a straw hat look unbelievably chic – the all-American girl has grown up.

Denim Shortall Cut-offs

THEN ADD:

black leather choker

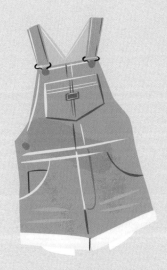

black combat boots

breezy open-neck
striped T-shirt

black leather
mini backpack

Denim Coveralls

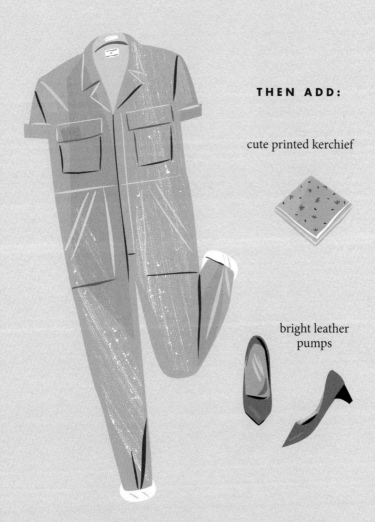

THEN ADD:

cute printed kerchief

bright leather
pumps

Vintage Denim Cut-off Shorts

THEN ADD:

worn vintage
T-shirt

Wayfarer sunglasses

fringe black
leather purse

black cowboy boots

23

Style Icon

STEVIE NICKS

egendary singer-songwriter Stevie Nicks (b. 1948) soundtracked the 70s, 80s, and beyond with her mystical folk-rock, gravely vocal stylings for Fleetwood Mac, and her own bestselling solo career. Her style – then and now – is all wafty scarves, feathered bangs, gauzy skirts, and worn-in denim styled up with bohemian trinkets, top hats, and certain witchy air. Think: walking dream-catcher.

At first, Stevie's costumes helped her battle stage fright – she would hide under the leather and lace and become someone else entirely, belting out the 'Mac's greatest hits to millions. But, as her confidence and fame grew, Stevie's onstage outfits became an essential part of her personal look.

Pore over images of Nicks' decades-long career and you'll see how denim – in all its variations – has played a key role in her style evolution. High waisted, wide leg, form-fitting jeans were her thing – nothing too revealing (Nicks loves to remain mysterious). And if you're in any doubt of Nicks' denim-love, just plug in your headphones and crank up her 1994 album *Street Angel*. The opening track is a steamy ode to a lost love called *Blue Denim*.

Distressed Denim Cut-off Shorts

THEN ADD:

silky kimono
jacket

simple white
tank top

witchy knee
high suede
boots

folksy crystal
necklaces

Stonewashed, Sleeveless Denim Vest

THEN ADD:

brimmed
felt hat

black cotton
jersey slip
dress

black
leather
tote

chunky
sunglasses

black leather
booties

29

Ripped White Denim Jeans

THEN ADD:

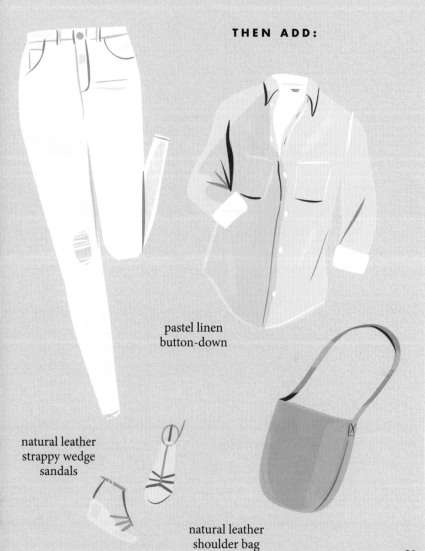

pastel linen
button-down

natural leather
strappy wedge
sandals

natural leather
shoulder bag

31

Style Icon

DEBBIE HARRY

The onetime waitress, go-go dancer, and Playboy Bunny, Debbie Harry (b. 1945) is the vocalist for New Wave band Blondie, celebrated art-house film actor, cult style hero, and lifelong denim aficionado.

Harry took to the stage in the mid-70s, already a key player in the NYC alternative scene. With musician Chris Stein, her ex-partner, Blondie gave the world a glimpse of the city's burgeoning creativity through a pop-rock lens – and boy did Harry look amazing. Bleached blonde hair, kohl eyes, razor-sharp cheek bones and double denim: slim-cut stonewash jeans, jackets worn as shirts, sleeveless denim vests, cute cut-offs to wear to Coney Island, worn with dark glasses, ripped up vintage sports tops and little leather jackets: it was a punk-edged look inspired by the streets, but unlike fellow all-American groups like the Ramones, there was an art-inspired, upbeat edge to Harry's style (and Blondie's music).

Many have fallen for Harry's unique way of dressing (and filthy wisecracks), including Andy Warhol to whom Harry was a friend and muse. Her 70s and 80s looks – completely unique at the time – are now so influential in contemporary fashion they seem timeless. Worn-in jeans, beautifully bashed up vintage denim jackets, cool shades, and thrift store tees: it's like we've been dressing as Deborah Harry forever – and we're all the better for it.

Flared, Cropped, Modern-Fit Overalls

THEN ADD:

fitted striped mock
turtleneck

strappy suede clogs

Cropped, Frayed Cuff Flares

THEN ADD:

denim
workwear
jacket

black
leather tote

black leather
booties

Knee-Length, Fitted Button-Front Jean Skirt

THEN ADD:

Western snap-front denim shirt

leather bucket bag

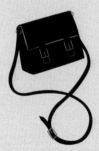

blue-tinted sunglasses

natural leather slip-on clogs

Style Icon

DREW BARRYMORE

Born inside the Hollywood machine, onetime child star Drew Barrymore (b. 1975) spent her childhood pretending to be someone else. From *E.T.* to *Never Been Kissed*, the irreverent, cute AF actor, director and producer (from the theatrical Barrymore family) has been part of our lives for three-plus decades, appearing in the movies that have shaped our world. After battling alcohol and drug abuse (read: *Little Girl Lost*, Drew's autobiography), it was in the 1990s that Drew truly shone out, creating an unstoppable career and her own influential style. Hers was a grunge-influenced waster look with chunky vintage denim at its core. She popped up at LA parties in high waisted mum jeans, slouchy dungarees and ripped up boyfriend denim with plaid shirts and crumpled tees worn with bleached blonde curls, blackberry lips, cute key chains and crucifix necklaces.

In 2009, Drew starred in *Grey Gardens*, a drama based on a cult documentary about two society shut-ins living in the Hamptons – and scored a slew of award nominations and her best reviews yet. Her red-carpet look became a little more slick and her personal style seemed sharper and more refined. Today, it's all about a chic, off-duty LA-look where Drew plays the part of the quirky, bohemian mother (she has two kids) and even designer (she has collaborated on a fashion collection with Amazon). Soft, threadbare vintage tees, skinny and slim jeans, and flipping elegantly between flip flops, Cons, and chunky platform heels; her uniform perfectly reflects this period of her life: confident, happy, and doesn't GAF.

Button-Front Full Denim Skirt

THEN ADD:

baby-rib
striped
bodysuit

vintage leather
shoulder bag

delicate gold
locket

strappy cotton
espadrilles

Oversized Shearling Denim Workwear Jacket

THEN ADD:

slim-fit black jeans

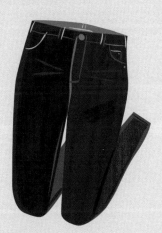

heather grey cashmere
crewneck

black canvas
slip-on sneakers

soft,
slouchy
knit hat

Oversized Vintage Denim Jacket

THEN ADD:

black porkpie
hat

black super
skinny jeans

round
sunglasses

black leather
mini backpack

white V-neck
T-shirt

combat boots

Style Icon

MISSY ELLIOTT

Hip-hop legend Missy Elliott (b. 1971) has worked for decades creating and performing some of finest contemporary pop music, singing, rapping and producing her was to icon status.

Most kids in the 90s and 00s were obsessed with music videos, and it's during this period that Elliott first hit our TV screens with her own unique sound and visual expression. She flipped between eye-popping tracksuits and double denim and seems to have the finest acrylics in the industry (have you seen those bejewelled bad boys?), something she's devoted salon time to since she was 16. Elliott formed all-female R&B outfit Fayze (later known as Sista) in the late 80s, moved into a house in New York shared by fellow artists on the Swing Mob imprint, and eventually helped form The Superfriends music collective with Timbaland, Ginuwine, Magoo and Playa.

Elliott's love of denim is loud and proud and more than a little showy: she's a fan of distressed, patched and embroidered double-denim looks peppered with applique, studs and sparkles, and matching accessories. There's something deliciously masculine about Elliott's style. It's a middle finger to the representation of many women in hip-hop music, and the antithesis of background bikini girls. Above all, it's a form of peacocking borrowed from the boys – and delivered back to them with jewels on.

Button-Fly Denim Cut-offs

THEN ADD:

cropped sport jersey

black leather bum bag

cute gold necklaces and
hoop earrings

sporty, strappy
black sandals

Ripped, Stonewashed Skinny Jeans

THEN ADD:

breton-striped boatneck

matching heels

refined, classic shoulder tote

Multi-Tone, Double-Breasted Denim Suit

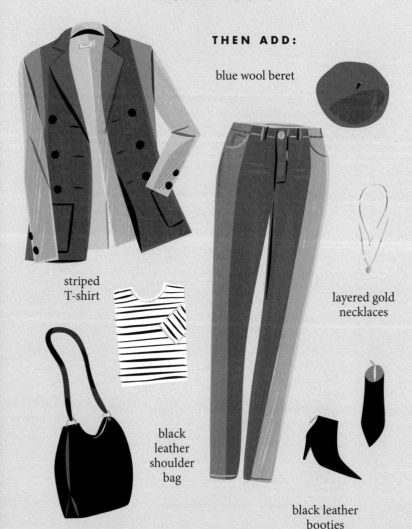

THEN ADD:

blue wool beret

striped T-shirt

layered gold necklaces

black leather shoulder bag

black leather booties

Style Icon

ZOË KRAVITZ

As the daughter of musician Lenny Kravitz and actor Lisa Bonet, Zoë Kravitz (b. 1988) has long had mag editors in a froth – and it's not just her lineage or celeb friend crew that excites. Her unique sense of style (and acting ability) has made Kravitz the ultimate girl crush, and it is vintage denim with a sweet, slow fade that plays a key part of her wardrobe.

On screen, Kravitz's look – goth babysitter, stripper-mutant, future revolutionary – is as eclectic as her off-screen persona. In *Fantastic Beasts: The Crimes of Grindlewald* she plays a glamourous, possibly dangerous witch in 1920s New York, and in *Big Little Lies*, an annoyingly perfect hippie yoga instructor.

Day-to-day, Kravitz often dresses with a 90s edge, her look is sometimes capricious, other times slick and considered. Sophisticated or vintage-powered looks work for upscale events, but Kravitz is just as likely to be dressed with a playful or sporty vibe. Her go-to is a vintage white T-shirt (she collects them) and delightfully worn-in jeans. There's a practical edge, too with cute flats, sneakers and bulging giant bags. Confident simplicity where Kravitz is at – she seems to simply wear whatever feels good, whatever the occasion, like slouching around in a pair of vintage jeans on the front row of the Saint Laurent show – and stealing the show.

Cropped, Slim Dark-Rinse Jeans

THEN ADD:

ruffled silk
statement top

artsy leather and
ceramic necklace

metallic silver heels

black leather
handbag

Distressed Bellbottom Jeans

folksy
peasant
blouse

natural leather satchel

rose-tinted
sunglasses

natural leather
platform shoes

Railroad-Striped Babydoll Dress

THEN ADD:

straw sun hat

white leather
exercise
sandals

canvas striped tote

Style Icon

JOYCE LEE

When J Crew chose Somsack Sikhounmuong, then the head of design for sister brand Madewell, to head up the preppy clothing label in 2015, it was LA-born Joyce Lee who took his place. Now head of design, Lee immediately put her own spin on the denim-focused brand. As Madewell's onetime accessories designer (and ex Marc Jacobs team member), Lee worked her way up through the ranks to be one of the world's most influential denim designers.

It's easy to underestimate the love Madewell fans have for Lee's take on the brand; her laidback, sophisticated, and 'accidentally cool' aesthetic has created an incredibly loyal following – think Brooklyn art student with an easy, LA boho edge.

Just as Lee's designs are beautiful and utilitarian, her own style is full of easy one-pieces, cute cotton shirt dresses, and a truckload of wonderfully worn-in jeans. Peppered with beads, simple accessories, and vintage finds (many from LA's legendary Rose Bowl Flea Market), Joyce's look crosses the eclectic/eccentric divide with just the right amount of wearable weirdness.

Oversized Pinstriped Denim Suit

THEN ADD:

black choker

chunky, white
hi-top sneakers

sporty, cotton
underwear set

Wide Leg, Dark-Rinse Denim Trousers

THEN ADD:

simple
geometric
necklace

khaki
trench
coat

classic, fitted
turtleneck sweater

black leather
handbag

black slingback heels

Dark-Rinse Skinny Jeans

THEN ADD:

bold, printed blouse

statement
necklace

brightly coloured clutch

black
suede clog
booties

Style Icon

AMY LEVERTON

Is there anyone who loves denim more than Amy Leverton? The LA-based indigo enthusiast (read: proud jeans geek) is the author of celebratory style tomes *Denim Dudes*, and *Denim: Street Style, Vintage, Obsession* and, as a trend forecaster, consultant and designer, Amy is the go-to for the world's finest denim brands and vintage dealers.

Amy worked for more than a decade in the denim and trend world, but it was the publication of *Denim Dudes* that marked her out as a key player in an often male-dominated industry. A real labour of love, the book has a contemporary street style focus on modern denim wearers (rather than a fusty historical focus); Amy now brings this hot take to her favourite brands, from techy denim producers to modern boutiques and vintage dealers.

What is it she loves most about denim? Apart from the wonderfully eccentric denimheads she meets and profiles, for Amy, it's the unique way the fabric fades and ages around the body, becoming a map of the wearer's life. As the woman behind many of your favourite contemporary denim trends, if you want to know about the future of denim and the very best of its past, get to know Amy.

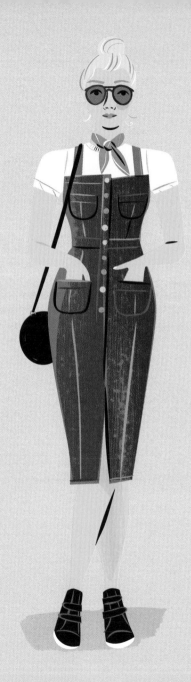

Fitted Denim Pencil Dress

THEN ADD:

white T-shirt

cute
sunglasses

cotton kerchief

round cross-body bag

black leather
hi-top sneakers

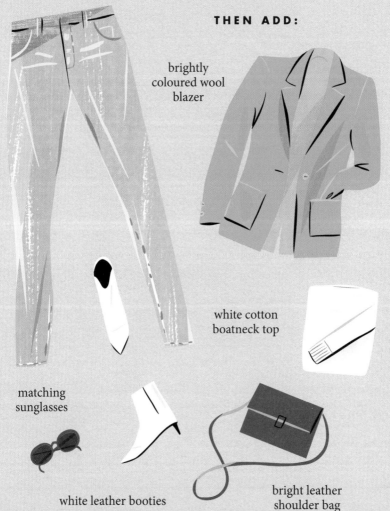

THEN ADD:

brightly
coloured wool
blazer

white cotton
boatneck top

matching
sunglasses

white leather booties

bright leather
shoulder bag

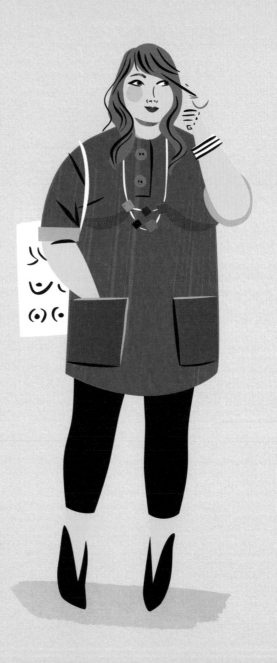

Structured Denim Tunic

bold, crafty
jewellery

silkscreened
canvas
tote bag

cropped
black
leggings

black leather
wedge heels

Style Icon

EMMYLOU HARRIS

If denim is the official uniform of the American West, then Country music is its soundtrack and Emmylou Harris is its queen. The winsome, willowy music and style icon (b. 1947) and college drop-out honed her craft in the coffee houses of New York in the folk music boom, but soon returned to her Alabama roots, singing country rock with the Flying Burrito Brothers. She has countless awards and a rich history of heart-aching harmonies and collabs with Dolly Parton, Linda Ronstadt, Neil Young, Bob Dylan, and Harris' greatest friend, Gram Parsons.

In the 70s and 80s, Emmylou Harris was faithfully Country before it was cool, wearing worn-in vintage denim with gorgeous fringed Western shirts and shawls, cowboy hats and gauzy, bohemian dresses. Her patched denim jackets, bootcut jeans, flares and skinnies (tucked into knee-high boots), and chunky mum jeans were the perfect Country look, accessorised with long, unstyled hair, a Gibson acoustic guitar with a leather strap monogrammed with her initials) and a choker-style ribbon around her neck. And boy did she look beautiful.

Even though Harris' career has spanned decades, her style has remained something of a constant (save the sequins and big hair of the 80s); it's a timeless and supremely wearable look. For Harris, there's been an enduring love of denim, a lot of country and a little rock and roll.

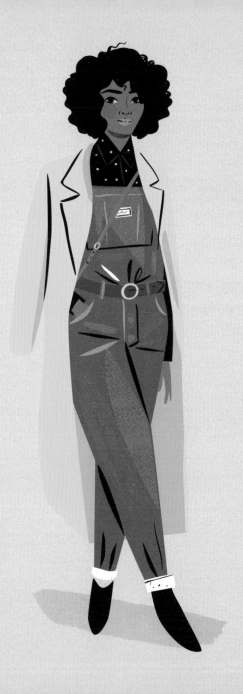

Boxy, Tapered Overalls

colourful
leather belt

pastel
wool
overcoat

swiss
dotted
blouse

black suede
booties

mini cross-body
satchel

83

Brightly-Coloured Denim Jeans

THEN ADD:

dark-rinse denim
button-down

sporty, colourful tote

crisp, white
sneakers

Denim Lace-Up Bikini

THEN ADD:

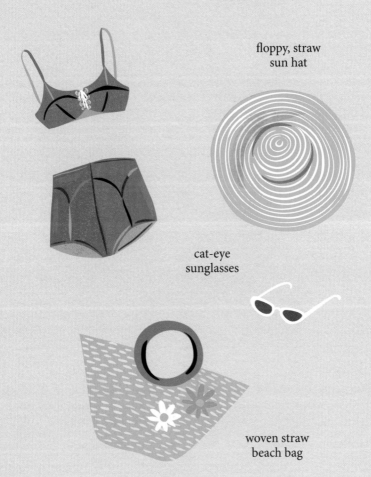

floppy, straw
sun hat

cat-eye
sunglasses

woven straw
beach bag

Style Icon

MARILYN MONROE

From the gust-up-the-gusset 'flying skirt' scene in *The Seven Year Itch* to the gold lame Travilla gown in *Gentlemen Prefer Blondes*, Monroe's double-denim outfit in *The Misfits* is perhaps one of her most heart-stopping looks. Born Norma Jeane Mortensen in 1926, the iconic performer from the golden age of Hollywood had grown up in LA foster homes, married at 16, and had a short career as a pin-up before hitting the big time. Portrayed as a bubble-headed blonde bombshell in many of her most successful films, in 1961 *The Misfits* broke with convention and gave a gravitas to Monroe's career. She died soon after.

James Dean wore a tee, leather jacket and jeans in *Rebel Without a Cause*, coining a new uniform for men who wanted to look completely different from their fathers – and embody Dean's subtly dangerous edge. In T*he Misfits*, Monroe did the same for women. Her slouchy blanket-lined denim jacket (the classic Storm Rider from denim brand, Lee®) and blue jeans were the antithesis of the cleavage-busting gowns Monroe had been known for – and was all the better for it. Photos from the set of the film – a dusty desert romance between recent divorce (Monroe) and an aging cowboy (Clark Gable) – are gorgeously realised. Monroe is sun-lit, denim-clad, and never looked more beautiful.

Button-Front, Dark-Rinse Shirtdress

THEN ADD:

opaque black tights

black leather
clutch

oxblood buckle
dress shoes

Raw-Edged, Denim Skirt Set

THEN ADD:

slim-fit white
tank top

dark indigo
head scarf

natural suede booties

FLEA MARKET FINDS

Are you a thrift store rummager? Or more of a Madewell-buyer? There's something enduringly magical about vintage denim: discover which brands to look out for when the flea market hits town.

Levi's® 501®

Levi's® 501® have changed little since the 1870s. Although contemporary versions are a little slimmer and more refined, the original men's fit is delightfully relaxed. Expect a button fly, a medium to long rise, rigid denim, straight leg with no taper, and 7 inch leg openings as standard. One of the most iconic jeans ever made.

Lee® Rider

Jeans-makers since 1889, it was in 1941 when Lee®'s popular cowboy pant was slimmed down to a more modern, wearable fit, known at the Lee® Rider 101. The genius behind the idea? Dancer Sally Rand who tweaked the brand's original design for her boyfriend, world champion saddle bronc rider Turk Greenough.

Fiorucci

'Denim is a love that never fades,' said Elio Fiorucci, creator of the first designer jeans. His fashion label took the humble workwear garment and made them chic, desirable, and oh-so-sexy. From his original Fiorucci store in Milan, he opened a series of crazy, cult boutiques throughout the 1970s in New York, Paris, London, LA, Sydney and Hong Kong.

Jordache®

Brooklyn brothers girl Joe, Ralph and Avi Nakash created cult denim brand Jordache in 1978 and it reigned throughout the 80s via its sexy, skinny fits and controversial advertising with lots of flesh (the brand's first big TV campaign – a topless woman riding a horse – was banned). It's now considered a valued vintage find, evoking the excesses of the decade. Wearing topless: optional.

OshKosh B'gosh®

Maker of sturdy work clothes since the late 1800s, US brand OshKosh B'gosh® had something of a heyday in the 1970s and 80s, dealing in wonderfully chunky overalls, bellbottoms and jeans. Now exclusively making children's clothing, adult OshKosh overalls are a cult thrift store favourite.

THE ART OF DENIM

First published in 2019 by Hardie Grant Books, an imprint of
Hardie Grant Publishing

Hardie Grant Books (UK)
52-54 Southwark Street
London SE1 1UN

Hardie Grant Books (Australia)
Ground Floor, Building 1
658 Church Street
Melbourne, VIC 3121

hardiegrantbooks.com

British Library Cataloguing-in-Publication Data. A catalogue
record for this book is available from the British Library.

ISBN: 978-1-78488-235-8

Publishing Director: Kate Pollard
Junior Editor: Eila Purvis
Illustrator: Libby VanderPloeg
Art Direction: Libby VanderPloeg
Colour Reproduction by p2d

Printed and bound in China
by Leo Paper Group

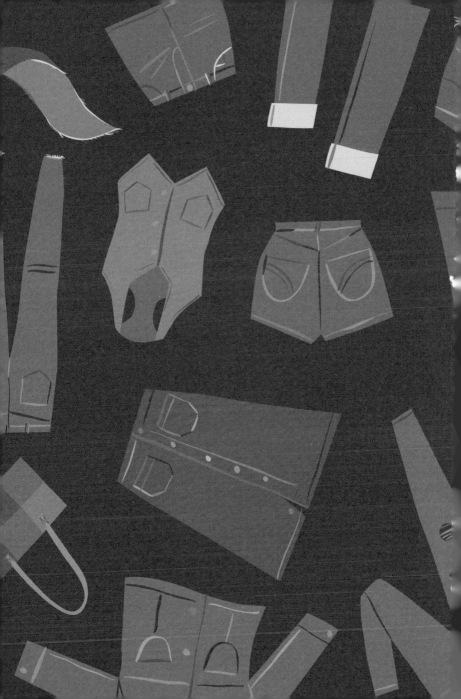